the color of roses

the color of roses

A Curated Spectrum of 300 Blooms

Danielle Dall'Armi Hahn

Photographs by Victoria Pearson

TEN SPEED PRESS

California | New York

Contents

*He who must have beautiful roses in his garden
must have beautiful roses in his heart.*

–S. REYNOLDS HOLE,
A BOOK ABOUT ROSES, 1880

Introduction

Many people have a strong memory of seeing and smelling their first rose. That's where this love affair started for me. I remember that day in my grandmother's garden and the rose—Sutter's Gold. It had the most beautiful fragrance and form, but, oh, what a color! It was an intriguing golden yellow with sepia undertones and outer petals where distinct veins of melon pink transitioned to russet at the edges. My grandmother was a rosarian, and her love for roses continues to inspire, guide, and encourage my own journey with this elegant flower.

When my husband and I met, we quickly discovered that our shared passion was the garden, and, specifically, the rose garden. Over the next ten years, we created several small personal rose gardens in our homes. When we arrived at our current farm more than thirty years ago, it was clear that we would need dozens of roses for the houses on the property, all built at the turn of the nineteenth century and crying out for romantic shrub roses in all colors of the rainbow.

In 1995, I entered my first rose exhibition. I came home with a few blue ribbons, which as a novice was completely unexpected. Not long after this modest success, visitors began stopping by to see our roses. One of them was a well-respected floral designer. He asked if he could cut a few roses for an arrangement someone had ordered. Rose Story Farm was born.

As we grew the farm, our thinking about rose selection evolved. Blocks of color in various shades and multiple varieties appealed to designers. As we developed our business selling cut flowers to the trade, our rose collection expanded. We now cut from more than 40,000 rose plants for the national floral trade and event design world. We began to host tours and educational seminars emphasizing the simplicity and ease of growing roses. There are a few simple guidelines that begin with the choice of a disease-resistant variety in a desirable color. As we had more visitors, we began to receive requests to design and maintain private gardens. We now maintain a nursery with rose plants that have been carefully curated for our garden clients. The plants we recommend for gardens are all fragrant, all good cutting varieties, and encompass a full range

of colors. A primary interest to all our clients (designers, gardeners, and rose enthusiasts) is color and how to choose roses within a desired color palette.

I take heart knowing that roses can be grown just about anywhere. All our children have roses around their homes, from an apartment balcony in Dublin, Ireland, where a single bloom of iceberg planted in a pot is doted on, to a small backyard in Houston, Texas, where a Julia Child rose pumps out the blooms, to Altadena, California, where our daughter and her husband have planted a serious rose garden that is a major focus of their spare time. We have clients across the country growing roses, many with unique challenges. But the challenges come with sweet rewards.

It has been a dream of mine to write a book about roses, sharing my love for these gorgeous beauties and demystifying them for both gardener and flower arranger. A great number of books about roses seem to emphasize their complexities and the difficulties encountered in their cultivation. My experience has been very different, and I appreciate the simple and straightforward nature of their place in our gardens and in our homes. I find roses easy to grow, easy to cut and arrange, and always gratifying.

The purpose of this book is to provide a reference and color guide for those choosing plants for their gardens, designing for a special event, planning for home floral arrangements, or simply dreaming about a future full of roses.

Roses and Color

Roses have been treasured for centuries. Romantic beauty, lovely fragrance, intriguing history, rich symbolic power, and amazing versatility are the touchstones of this plant. They bloom from spring until frost, in virtually all but the most frigid garden zones. There is a great range of varieties to suit everyone. It's no wonder they are one of the world's most popular flowers. One of their most extraordinary features is the nearly endless array of color options. You would be hard pressed to find another flower with such color diversity.

When using roses in your garden and in your home, color is of primary importance. Color sets the mood. Our reaction to color is personal and emotional. Colors are often divided into warm and cool colors: reds, yellows, and oranges are warm colors; while greens, blues, and violets are cool. One simple design approach for a garden or a floral arrangement is to focus on all warm or all cool tones. Another option, as shown below, is to use harmonizing colors together. These are adjacent to each other on the color wheel; for example, red with orange, orange with yellow, or yellow with green. Or one can try using contrasting colors together, which

lie opposite each other on the color wheel, such as violet with yellow or red with green. When using contrasting color, I suggest choosing one primary color, and using the second color sparingly as an accent. When transitioning from one area to another, use white or other color blenders in neutral tones. White can be used to separate areas as well, either intentionally or incidentally.

Roses come in a remarkable array of colors from single tones to subtle blends. From the deepest golds and coppers to the buff tones of yellow to striking reds and oranges, breeders are constantly increasing the numbers of hues and combinations or blends of colors. There is an advantage to using blended colors in roses as they coordinate with both colors in the bloom. For instance, the Peace rose, which is a yellow and pink blend, coordinates beautifully with both yellows and pinks. And finally, do not forget about fun and exuberant colors (some are almost fluorescent), bicolors, and various striped or multicolor roses. These can be used either as a focus point or an accent in both gardens and flower arrangements.

Roses in the Landscape

Roses can be seen as artistry in nature. Surely, Louise Beebe Wilder had roses in mind when she wrote, "In his garden, every man may be his own artist without apology or explanation" (*Colour in My Garden*, 1918). Few home gardens have the luxury of being arranged strictly for artistic color effects. Most gardens develop over time, but even if one is only adding a new feature to an established garden, color should be considered a primary interest. As you are choosing roses for your landscape, consider the paint color and materials of your house. Use harmonizing colors when selecting roses to plant next to your home. With natural materials, such as stone, brick, and wood, just about any color works. With brick, for instance,

Left: Contrasting colors in an arrangement.
Right: Harmonious colors in an arrangement.

use pinks, yellows, or even a contrasting color such as lavender. When choosing rose colors for a painted wall, use more saturated tones. Select a color that is close to the wall color but deeper, making sure the rose color is dominant, not the wall color.

Pure bright colors have energy and are exciting. They are the first to catch our eye, calling attention to themselves. They are easy to select, but a word of caution: use thoughtfully and with restraint, as a little goes a very long way. In a large garden, masses of bright color may be dramatic but in smaller settings, as they may be overwhelming and distracting. Bright colors can be used as accent or focal points. Just a few red, orange, or yellow blooms will liven up a planting bed of muted or softer colors. Using these colors as screens can be helpful as they easily hide imperfections in the garden.

Create a color scheme around a few plants in a single hot color. Think light pink or coral with a touch of red or apricot and pale yellow with a pop of bright orange. These combinations are vivid and stimulating, evocative of a sunrise or sunset. In truth, they are seen best in full sunlight.

Meanwhile, cool colors create depth and can make a garden appear larger and more expansive. Cool colors are restful and reparative. In nature they are found in the sky, in the ocean, and in the distance. Pastel shades are the easiest to work with in landscape. They are soft yet bright and they soothe the eye. White, or very light-colored roses, can be cooling, meditative, or spectacular, and perhaps are best enjoyed in the evening or in the moonlight.

The color of your roses will change due to the difference in light throughout the day. Early morning light, midday light, and sunset light will all contribute to the variation in colors in your garden.

For cutting gardens, no rules apply, since these beds of flowers are grown specifically for cutting and use in floral arrangements, not for their landscaping attributes. Designate an area that can be easily changed or amended when new colors catch your interest. Plant colors you like and that complement your home interior. Also consider roses that can be cut and gifted. There is nothing sweeter than a rose bouquet cut from a home garden.

Roses in Flower Arranging

When choosing roses for flower arrangements, consider the setting and purpose for the arrangement. Are you creating arrangements for your home, creating a centerpiece for a dinner party, planning your wedding, or perhaps choosing a bouquet to gift a friend? I suggest you start with a color that you like and go from there.

Pastel tones are beautiful in a springtime bouquet or in less formal settings. Contrasting colors can be dramatic and more formal, as can gem tones and deeper shades within one color palette. These deeper shades tend to be more formal and opulent. White is always elegant and formal. Likewise, single-color arrangements can be dramatic and formal, though darker colors are safest when a formal look is desired. Mixing textures (consider petal count and stages of bloom, as pictured top left on page 11) and harmonizing colors create a less formal or more friendly feel.

For house arrangements, dinner parties, and gifting, using darker shades within a color family (rather than clear tones) is a safe choice. Roses with sepia tones are easiest to match to wall coverings and furnishings. These would be off-tones of colors, such as cream, dusty yellow, or tan (as pictured top right, opposite), and lavender, mauve, or deep russet. As a starting point, match rose colors to fabric or paint samples. You might also choose seasonal colors or colors for holidays. For spring, choose pastels. Fall yearns for sunset and russet tones. Pure whites and jewel tones suit the holidays.

In tablescapes, bright colors can conceal flaws or be used when budgets are tight (more greenery, fewer blooms). Be particularly careful when choosing pinks and yellows. Pinks with a dash of orange work better than pinks with blue hues. Dark yellow or gold may be a better choice than a lemon yellow, because these are not pure color tones and pure tones are harder to match.

When designing for an event, floral design trends and color themes change as often as fashion. However, basic design premises remain unchanged. Just as in landscapes, floral arrangements can use harmonizing or contrasting colors. Harmonizing colors, or those close to each other on the color wheel, are easiest to use as they tend to blend with little or no effort. When blending, choose colors close on the color wheel and blend with varying shades of each. An example of this would be apricot and peach, mixed with light pinks containing a tinge of orange (as pictured on bottom left, opposite) as opposed to "blue" pinks (as pictured on bottom right, opposite).

Contrasting colors, such as purples and yellows, are a bit more of a challenge and can appear "polka dotty" if care is not used to bridge the two colors. When using contrasting colors, choose a bicolor or blended rose in similar colors to bridge. Take care to choose the less "clear" or "pure" colors or "off" shades when using contrasting colors. The sepia tones in the rose color will be the blending factor.

How to Use this Book

Choosing three hundred roses for this book was no easy feat. First and foremost, I wanted a good representation of all major colors, because color remains the single most important aspect of rose choice. But shape, plant growth habit, ease of cultivation, fragrance, and remontancy (repeat blooming) have a role and were considered in my decisions. Most of the roses included are readily available as either plants or cut stems of roses.

While there are more than three thousand different rose varieties in commerce today, this book focuses mainly on "modern roses," which are technically those hybridized after 1867. Many older roses are still available, but the more recently developed roses have the advantage of repeat blooming throughout the year, improved disease resistance, glorious and subtle color combinations, improved vase life, and incredible fragrance.

Modern roses come in every color except blue. The older roses included in this book, such as Sombreuil (page 31) and Mlle Cécile Brünner (page 288), have unique qualities which make them extremely special. Both have many characteristics shared by modern roses, such as remontancy and disease resistance. Sombreuil is a heavily petaled, flat quartered white flower with a growth habit that makes it a lovely choice for climbing into and over structures, such as arches or gazebos. Mlle Cécile Brünner is a prolific climber that can be used as a dominant fixture in landscaping. Its long, arching canes are terrific in floral arrangements and the tiny pink fragranced blooms are unique in the rose world.

Try not to get your heart set on one particular rose. Choose several roses in a

color that you like so that you are not disappointed if your rose of choice is not available. Roses in commerce are determined by what sells, and what sells can vary from year to year. Fashion trends change, so do rose selections. If you find yourself choosing a rose that is not currently available, talk to your nursery about saving one for you when their new stock arrives. If it is no longer available in commerce, make sure that your nursery knows you are looking. Not only will they be able to notify you if they are able to find the variety, but they can convey your thoughts and wish lists to the actual rose growers. With enough interest, a rose can be brought back into commerce.

If you are choosing by color, your local nursery can suggest a good variety in the color you want that will thrive in your garden zone. As you become more comfortable growing roses, you can experiment with other varieties, perhaps choosing not only for color, but for shape, size, and fragrance. Use this book to choose color combinations, play with the outcomes on paper, and have fun. Nothing is permanent in nature, so don't be afraid to experiment with different colors and patterns. If you are not satisfied with the result, move things around and try again. Make it your own.

The photographs in this book are untouched. The photographer and I have included the leaves where we feel they are integral to the beauty of the individual rose. You will see an occasional insect, or evidence of insect damage and/or disease, such as on pages 8, 12, and 19. We have attempted to show the beauty of the bloom in nature and not focus on perfection. Gardening teaches us patience and acceptance. Perfection has no place in a garden. Instagram, with all its filters, has skewed our perceptions of beauty. Disappointment is inevitable if one continues to strive for flawlessness.

Do not expect that the color of an individual rose will match any photograph or visual reproduction. The color of a particular rose variety is never static and never exact. For example, a blossom of Fair Bianca (page 29), although always white, will vary slightly based on the particulars of cultivation, including soil composition, moisture content, duration of sunlight exposure, temperature, soil microbiome, and plant age. Colors inevitably lighten in the dog days of summer, and then intensify in the fall. As an individual bloom opens and matures, its inherent color will reveal itself slowly and then gradually fade as it is spent. These realities may be either frustrating or exciting, endearing or difficult, but should never be unexpected.

While we have chosen not to include petal count as part of the individual rose descriptions, do take note of the petals in a single bloom while perusing the rose photographs. In the garden, roses with a large petal

count (more than forty petals) typically need a warmer climate to fully open. Likewise, roses with fewer petals (sixteen or fewer petals) may do better in cooler climates due to their more fragile nature. In flower arranging, single petal roses or roses with a small petal count provide a unique texture to arrangements. The stamens in the interior of the rose will almost always be visible in a fully open, single petal bloom or in a bloom with low petal count. Likewise, a bloom with high petal count will virtually never be open enough to see the stamens. The current trend in flower arranging is fewer blooms with more distinct visible features in each bloom. Massed arrangements call for higher petal count roses completely filling the container and leaving no negative space.

In the captions for the rose photography on pages 22 to 321, the following information is provided for each rose.

Name

Most roses have a scientific name as well as a commercially accepted name. I have chosen to use just the commercial name used in the US.

Breeder

As you gain experience growing roses, you will begin learning to associate specific breeders with certain rose characteristics. For example, David Austin varieties tend to be shrubs and can be expected to be vigorous and disease resistant. The Meilland varieties inevitably have fragrance, but tend to fall into the hybrid tea categories, so they will grow taller with straighter stems. Kordes roses, in general, have less fragrance; however, they tend to last longer in the vase as they have a firmer petal. Many of the American hybridizers have combined the best of these features, particularly in the varieties they have developed in the last ten years. Most roses that have been hybridized or developed in Europe are relatively disease resistant because European pesticide regulations traditionally have been more restrictive than in the US. However, in the past thirty years, as Americans have become focused on the environment, organic practices have become more important. Consequently, American breeders have recently focused on developing more disease-resistant roses. Always refer to rose catalogs for more precise information on the characteristics of the plant and flower before making your decisions.

Year of Earliest Introduction

If you are a novice rose grower, look for the color you like, then choose among roses that have been bred in the past thirty years. These tend to be the most disease resistant.

Type

There is much information to be gleaned by the type or category of the rose, such as plant growth habit, overall plant size, stem strength, and length, and in many instances, shape of the bloom. The roses I have chosen to include in the book primarily fall into the following categories.

Hybrid tea roses: A single bloom on longer, stronger stems and tends to grow more upright. Most are three to four feet tall, although some can grow as tall as eight feet. Commonly seen in more formal gardens.

Floribunda roses: Multiple blooms on a single stem. The plants tend to grow a bit wider and stay slightly smaller than hybrid tea roses. Most are twenty-four to forty-eight inches tall. Excellent in cutting gardens due to their prolific blooms.

Grandiflora roses: A combination of hybrid tea size with floribunda habit—both multiple blooms on a single stem and a wider plant. These make spectacular anchoring for the back of garden beds with smaller rose varieties in the forefront.

Shrub roses: Just as it sounds, these tend to grow like shrubs, with multiple stems growing in multiple directions, all with plentiful blooms. They typically look bushy and are not as well defined as other types of roses, which tend to have fewer, more prominent canes. These roses are typically easier to care for than other rose varieties and do well in informal or cottage garden settings.

Climber roses: Strong, vigorous roses with blooms of varying sizes and long, flexible canes that will climb a supporting structure. For simplicity's sake, I have taken the liberty of classifying some old garden roses as "old climbers." They have the same attributes as modern climbers and are predominantly remontant,

disease resistant, and vigorous. Technically, they belong to a subgroup of "old garden roses." For more information, please see our website, www.rosestoryfarm.com.

Miniature, miniflora, and hybrid China roses: Miniatures have been selectively bred to stay small in size, have smaller flowers than standard rose bushes, and are extremely hardy. The relatively new class of minifloras (since 1999) was developed for bushes with bloom and plant size between miniatures and floribundas. Hybrid China plants (see The Green Rose, page 53) are part of the old garden rose classification. They are generally small (two to three feet tall), remontant, not particularly hardy, and require winter protection in cold climates.

Fragrance

Many gardeners look for fragrance when choosing a rose. For the production of hydrosols or perfumes from roses, look for the most fragrant varieties. However, if a rose is to be used in a food setting, too much fragrance can be a nuisance. There is a trade-off: less fragrant roses typically have thicker petals, resulting in a prolonged vase life. Petals contain fragrance pores, and thinner petals translate to more fragrance pores. That is why "grocery store" roses (with leather-like petals), have no fragrance, but can last weeks in a vase.

Fragrance is noted as slight, moderate, or strong. In the case where I've included roses with no fragrance, it is because the color is spectacular.

Plant Size

I've included plant size as an aid to help you plan your garden. Size varies depending on your climate and garden zone. Plant sizes noted are based loosely on plants grown in USDA Zones 6 to 7. For cooler climates, reduce the plant size by approximately 10 to 15 percent. Likewise, in warmer climates, plant size can increase by 10 to 15 percent. Plant

> **Plant size is noted as (height by width):**
> Small: 2 to 3 feet by 2 to 3 feet
> Medium: 3 to 5 feet by 3 to 5 feet
> Large: larger than 5 feet by 5 feet (except for climbers, whose spread may not be as wide as 5 feet)

size is also affected by fertilizer, available nutrients, and water content, as well as sun and wind exposure. Most importantly, plants can be kept at any desired size with proper pruning.

Bloom Size

I've included bloom size to assist you in choosing roses for cutting and floral arranging. Large blooms cannot be used in most tablescapes, due to space considerations, but can be lovely in large-scale installations. A smaller bloom can be used in multiple settings, as filler or texture or as a primary focus flower in bouquets or arrangements.

Bloom size is noted as:
Small: 1 to 2 inches
Medium: 2 to 3.5 inches
Large: 3.5 to 5 inches
Very large: larger than 5 inches

For gardeners, bloom size, while of less importance than in floral design, does need special mention in certain circumstances, particularly when choosing climbing roses. If choosing a large-bloom climber to grow on a structure, the structure needs to be strong enough to support the larger blooms. Many of the older climbing varieties, while vigorous in growth habit, tend to have smaller blossoms and bloom less frequently. These can be chosen for less formal areas and where more overall coverage is desired. The newer, large-blossomed climbers demand attention and provide a wonderful background for a more formal setting. Keep in mind that bloom size can also change depending on your garden zone or seasonally within your zone. For instance, spring blooms tend to be significantly larger than fall blooms.

For more information, please refer to our website: www.rosestoryfarm.com. Here you will find current resources, helpful gardening tips, as well as additional notes about each rose variety.

300 Roses

Jardins de Bagatelle
Meilland, 1986
Hybrid tea • Strong fragrance
Medium plants • Large blooms

Bolero
Meilland, 1998
Hybrid tea • Strong fragrance
Small plants • Medium blooms

Sally Holmes

Holmes, 1976
Shrub • Slight fragrance
Large plants • Medium blooms

Madame Alfred Carrière
Schwartz, 1879
Old climber • Strong fragrance
Large plants • Medium blooms

25

Easy Spirit
Carruth, 2017
Floribunda • Slight fragrance
Medium plants • Large blooms

26

Martine Guillot
Guillot-Massad, 1996
Shrub • Strong fragrance
Large plants • Large blooms

27

Desdemona
Austin, 2016
Shrub • Strong fragrance
Medium plants • Medium blooms

Fair Bianca
Austin, 1982
Shrub • Strong fragrance
Medium plants • Medium blooms

Winchester Cathedral
Austin, 1988
Shrub • Moderate fragrance
Medium plants • Medium blooms

Sombreuil
Robert, 1880
Climber • Moderate fragrance
Medium plants • Medium blooms

Classic Woman
Meilland, 2008
Hybrid tea • Slight fragrance
Medium plants • Large blooms

White Majesty
Meilland, 2006
Hybrid tea • Slight fragrance
Medium plants • Large blooms

Susan Williams-Ellis
Austin, 2011
Shrub • Moderate fragrance
Medium plants • Medium blooms

Shirley's Bouquet
Orard, 2015
Hybrid tea • Strong fragrance
Medium plants • Large blooms

John F. Kennedy
Boerner, 1965
Hybrid tea • Moderate fragrance
Medium plants • Very large blooms

White Veranda
Kordes, 2020
Floribunda • Slight fragrance
Small plants • Medium blooms

Sugar Moon
Bédard, 2010
Hybrid Tea • Strong fragrance
Medium plants • Large blooms

41

Gourmet Popcorn
Desamero, 1986
Miniature • Slight fragrance
Small plants • Small blooms

43

Windermere
Austin, 2007
Shrub • Moderate fragrance
Medium plants • Medium blooms

Pillow Fight
Carruth, 1999
Shrub • Strong fragrance
Small plants • Small blooms

Claire Austin
Austin, 2008
Shrub • Strong fragrance
Medium plants • Medium blooms

Lichfield Angel
Austin, 2007
Shrub • Slight fragrance
Large plants • Large blooms

49

French Lace
Warriner, 1980
Floribunda • Slight fragrance
Medium plants • Medium blooms

Green Romantica
Meilland, 2008
Hybrid tea • Slight fragrance
Medium plants • Large blooms

The Green Rose (*Rosa viridiflora*)
Bambridge & Harrison, 1845
Hybrid China • Slight fragrance
Small plants • Medium blooms

Limoncello
Meilland, 2008
Shrub • Slight fragrance
Medium plants • Medium blooms

Malvern Hills
Austin, 2001
Climber • Slight fragrance
Medium plants • Small blooms

Casino
McGredy, 1963
Climber • Strong fragrance
Large plants • Large blooms

57

Tottering-by-Gently

Austin, 2019
Shrub • Slight fragrance
Medium plants • Medium blooms

Vanessa Bell
Austin, 2018
Shrub • Moderate fragrance
Medium plants • Medium blooms

Lemon Spice
Armstrong/Swim, 1966
Hybrid tea • Strong fragrance
Medium plants • Large blooms

The Pilgrim
Austin, 1993
Shrub • Moderate fragrance
Large plants • Large blooms

62

Peace
Meilland, 1945
Hybrid tea • Moderate fragrance
Medium plants • Large blooms

St. Patrick
Strickland, 1995
Hybrid tea • Slight fragrance
Medium plants • Large blooms

Doris Day
Bédard, 2013
Floribunda • Strong fragrance
Medium plants • Large blooms

Imogen

Austin, 2017
Shrub • Slight fragrance
Medium plants • Medium blooms

Life of the Party
Carruth, 2018
Floribunda • Strong fragrance
Small plants • Medium blooms

Moonlight Romantica
Meilland, 2018
Hybrid tea • Strong fragrance
Large plants • Large blooms

Winter Sun
Kordes, 2009
Hybrid tea • Slight fragrance
Medium plants • Medium blooms

Michelangelo
Meilland, 1997
Hybrid tea • Slight fragrance
Medium plants • Large blooms

Sutter's Gold
Swim, 1950
Hybrid tea • Strong fragrance
Medium plants • Large blooms

Teasing Georgia
Austin, 1998
Shrub • Moderate fragrance
Large plants • Large blooms

Golden Opportunity
Weeks, 2020
Climber • Moderate fragrance
Large plants • Large blooms

Rio Samba
Warriner, 1991
Hybrid tea • Slight fragrance
Large plants • Large blooms

80

Gold Medal
Christensen, 1982
Grandiflora • Slight fragrance
Medium plants • Large blooms

Sunshine Daydream
Meilland, 2012
Grandiflora • Slight fragrance
Medium plants • Medium blooms

84

Sol Desire
Texas Rose Ventures, 2015
Floribunda • Slight fragrance
Small plants • Medium blooms

South Africa
Kordes, 2001
Grandiflora • Strong fragrance
Medium plants • Large blooms

Sultry
Zary, 2000
Hybrid tea • Slight fragrance
Large plants • Large blooms

87

Butterscotch
Warriner, 1986
Climber • Slight fragrance
Large plants • Medium blooms

Crocus Rose
Austin, 2001
Shrub • Slight fragrance
Medium plants • Medium blooms

Bright & Shiny
Radler, 2020
Floribunda • Slight fragrance
Medium plants • Medium blooms

Princesse Charlene de Monaco
Meilland, 2013
Hybrid tea • Strong fragrance
Medium plants • Large blooms

Wollerton Old Hall
Austin, 2012
Shrub • Strong fragrance
Medium plants • Medium blooms

Cream Veranda
Kordes, 2007
Floribunda • Moderate fragrance
Small plants • Medium blooms

Sespe Sunrise
Kordes, 2021
Hybrid tea • Strong fragrance
Medium plants • Medium blooms

Apricots n' Cream
Meilland, 2014
Hybrid tea • Slight fragrance
Large plants • Large blooms

The Lark Ascending
Austin, 2013
Shrub • Slight fragrance
Large plants • Medium blooms

Elle
Meilland, 2000
Hybrid tea • Strong fragrance
Medium plants • Large blooms

Medallion
Warriner, 1973
Hybrid tea • Slight fragrance
Medium plants • Very large blooms

105

Pegasus
Austin, 1995
Shrub • Strong fragrance
Medium plants • Medium blooms

Brandy
Swim/Christensen, 1981
Hybrid tea • Slight fragrance
Medium plants • Large blooms

Evelyn
Austin, 1991
Shrub • Strong fragrance
Medium plants • Large blooms

109

Colette
Meilland, 1994
Climber • Strong fragrance
Large plants • Medium blooms

Abraham Darby
Austin, 1985
Shrub • Strong fragrance
Medium plants • Large blooms

Chicago Peace
Johnston, 1962
Hybrid tea • Slight fragrance
Large plants • Large blooms

Sunset Celebration
Fryer, 1994
Hybrid tea • Strong fragrance
Medium plants • Large blooms

114

115

116

Edith's Darling
Bédard, 2016
Shrub • Strong fragrance
Small plants • Medium blooms

Fun in the Sun
Bédard, 2020
Grandiflora • Strong fragrance
Medium plants • Large blooms

Enchanted Peace
Meilland, 2020
Hybrid tea • Moderate fragrance
Medium plants • Medium blooms

119

Valencia
Kordes, 1989
Hybrid tea • Strong fragrance
Small plants • Large blooms

Marilyn Monroe
Carruth, 2002
Hybrid tea • Slight fragrance
Large plants • Large blooms

Bronze Star
Weeks, 2000
Hybrid tea • Strong fragrance
Large plants • Very large blooms

Port Sunlight
Austin, 2008
Shrub • Moderate fragrance
Medium plants • Medium blooms

Carding Mill

Austin, 2005
Shrub • Moderate fragrance
Medium plants • Medium blooms

Apricot Candy
Meilland, 2007
Hybrid tea · Moderate fragrance
Medium plants · Large blooms

127

Tropical Lightning
Orard, 2016
Climber • Slight fragrance
Large plants • Large blooms

Distant Drums
Buck, 1984
Shrub • Moderate fragrance
Medium plants • Medium blooms

Gemini
Zary, 1999
Hybrid tea • Slight fragrance
Large plants • Large blooms

131

First Prize
Boerner, 1970
Hybrid tea • Moderate fragrance
Large plants • Very large blooms

132

Pink Flamingo
Meilland, 2010
Grandiflora • Moderate fragrance
Medium plants • Large blooms

Love & Peace
Lim/Twomey, 2001
Hybrid tea • Moderate fragrance
Medium plants • Very large blooms

134

Elegant Lady
Zary, 1998
Hybrid tea • Slight fragrance
Medium plants • Large blooms

Shot Silk
Knight, 1931
Climber • Strong fragrance
Medium plants • Medium blooms

Sweet Mademoiselle
Meilland, 2017
Hybrid tea • Strong fragrance
Large plants • Large blooms

Dream Weaver
Zary, 1996
Climber • Moderate fragrance
Large plants • Medium blooms

Hot Cocoa
Carruth, 2002
Floribunda • Moderate fragrance
Medium plants • Medium blooms

143

Rosarium Uetersen
Kordes, 1977
Climber • Moderate fragrance
Large plants • Large blooms

Fragrant Cloud
Tantau, 1967
Hybrid tea • Strong fragrance
Small plants • Large blooms

Spice Twice
Zary, 1997
Hybrid tea · Strong fragrance
Medium plants · Large blooms

Jump for Joy
Bédard, 2013
Floribunda • Slight fragrance
Medium plants • Medium blooms

Lady Emma Hamilton
Austin, 2006
Shrub • Strong fragrance
Medium plants • Medium blooms

Sierra Lady
Kordes, 2016
Floribunda • Slight fragrance
Medium plants • Medium blooms

152

Crazy Love
Kordes, 2014
Shrub • Moderate fragrance
Medium plants • Large blooms

Oranges 'n' Lemons
McGredy, 1992
Shrub • Slight fragrance
Medium plants • Large blooms

Chihuly
Carruth, 2003
Floribunda • Slight fragrance
Medium plants • Medium blooms

Jean Giono
Meilland, 1994
Hybrid tea • Moderate fragrance
Medium plants • Large blooms

About Face
Carruth, 2004
Grandiflora • Slight fragrance
Medium plants • Large blooms

Chris Evert
Carruth, 1996
Hybrid tea • Moderate fragrance
Medium plants • Large blooms

159

Gingersnap
Delbard-Chabert, 1978
Floribunda • Slight fragrance
Small plants • Small blooms

Playboy
Cocker, 1976
Floribunda • Slight fragrance
Medium plants • Large blooms

Burst of Joy
Bédard, 2019
Floribunda • Slight fragrance
Medium plants • Medium blooms

Remember Me
Cocker, 1984
Hybrid tea • Slight fragrance
Small plants • Large blooms

Singin' in the Rain
McGredy, 1991
Floribunda • Moderate fragrance
Medium plants • Medium blooms

Light My Fire
Zary, 2008
Floribunda • Slight fragrance
Small plants • Medium blooms

Mojave
Swim, 1954
Hybrid tea • Moderate fragrance
Medium plants • Large blooms

Sheila's Perfume
Sheridan, 1982
Floribunda • Strong fragrance
Medium plants • Medium blooms

Flutterbye
Carruth, 1995
Shrub • Slight fragrance
Medium plants • Medium blooms

Joseph's Coat
Armstrong/Swim, 1963
Climber • Slight fragrance
Large plants • Large blooms

Perfect Moment
Kordes, 1989
Hybrid tea • Slight fragrance
Medium plants • Large blooms

173

Tangerine Streams
Bagnasco, 2011
Floribunda • Slight fragrance
Medium plants • Medium blooms

Rainbow Sorbet
Lim, 2006
Floribunda • Slight fragrance
Medium plants • Medium blooms

All American Magic
Meilland, 2008
Grandiflora • Slight fragrance
Medium plants • Medium blooms

177

Ketchup & Mustard
Bédard, 2011
Floribunda • Moderate fragrance
Medium plants • Medium blooms

François Rabelais
Meilland, 1996
Floribunda • Slight fragrance
Small plants • Medium blooms

Dolly Parton
Winchel, 1983
Hybrid tea • Strong fragrance
Medium plants • Large blooms

Legends
Carruth, 2007
Hybrid tea • Slight fragrance
Medium plants • Very large blooms

Double Delight
Swim/Ellis, 1977
Hybrid tea • Strong fragrance
Medium plants • Large blooms

Gypsy Soul
Kordes, 2016
Hybrid tea • Moderate fragrance
Small plants • Large blooms

L. D. Braithwaite
Austin, 1988
Shrub • Strong fragrance
Medium plants • Large blooms

Neil Diamond
Carruth, 2013
Hybrid tea • Strong fragrance
Medium plants • Large blooms

Olympiad
McGredy, 1982
Hybrid tea • Slight fragrance
Medium plants • Large blooms

Oklahoma
Swim/Weeks, 1964
Hybrid tea • Strong fragrance
Medium plants • Large blooms

Opening Night
Zary, 1998
Hybrid tea • Slight fragrance
Medium plants • Large blooms

188

Preference
Meilland, 2004
Floribunda • Slight fragrance
Small plants • Medium blooms

Red Eden
Meilland, 2003
Climber • Moderate fragrance
Large plants • Large blooms

Let Freedom Ring
Earman, 2004
Hybrid tea • Slight fragrance
Medium plants • Large blooms

Forever Yours
Tantau, 2018
Hybrid tea • Moderate fragrance
Medium plants • Large blooms

194

Mister Lincoln
Swim/Weeks, 1964
Hybrid tea • Strong fragrance
Medium plants • Large blooms

195

196

Love's Promise
Meilland, 1991
Hybrid tea • Strong fragrance
Small plants • Large blooms

Blaze
Kallay, 1932
Climber • Slight fragrance
Large plants • Small blooms

Love at First Sight

Bédard, 2019

Hybrid tea • Slight fragrance
Medium plants • Medium blooms

Crimson Bouquet
Kordes, 1999
Grandiflora • Slight fragrance
Medium plants • Large blooms

201

Ink Spots
Weeks, 1985
Hybrid tea • Slight fragrance
Medium plants • Large blooms

Isabel Renaissance
Poulsen, 1995
Shrub • Moderate fragrance
Medium plants • Large blooms

203

Black Magic
Tantau, 1997
Hybrid tea • Slight fragrance
Medium plants • Medium blooms

Dancing in the Dark
Delbard, 2006
Shrub • Slight fragrance
Medium plants • Medium blooms

Canyon Road
Meilland, 2015
Floribunda • Slight fragrance
Small plants • Medium blooms

Princess Anne
Austin, 2011
Shrub • Moderate fragrance
Medium plants • Large blooms

Della Reese
Bédard, 2020
Hybrid tea • Strong fragrance
Medium plants • Large blooms

Princess Alexandra Renaissance
Olesen, 1997
Shrub • Strong fragrance
Medium plants • Large blooms

Yves Piaget
Meilland, 1985
Hybrid tea • Strong fragrance
Medium plants • Large blooms

Deja Blu
Benardella, 2008
Miniflora • Moderate fragrance
Small plants • Medium blooms

Miranda Lambert
Texas Rose Ventures, 2014
Hybrid tea • Strong fragrance
Medium plants • Large blooms

Highwire Flyer
Radler, 2018
Climber • Slight fragrance
Large plants • Large blooms

Girls' Night Out

Meilland, 2010
Hybrid tea • Moderate fragrance
Medium plants • Large blooms

Sweet Spirit
Meilland, 2018
Grandiflora • Strong fragrance
Medium plants • Medium blooms

Pretty in Pink Eden
Tomerlin, 2015
Climber • Slight fragrance
Large plants • Large blooms

All My Loving
Fryer, 2011
Hybrid tea • Moderate fragrance
Small plants • Large blooms

Voluptuous!
Zary, 2005
Hybrid tea • Moderate fragrance
Medium plants • Large blooms

Love
Warriner, 1980
Grandiflora • Slight fragrance
Small plants • Large blooms

Chrysler Imperial
Lammerts, 1952
Hybrid tea • Strong fragrance
Medium plants • Large blooms

223

Elizabeth Taylor
Weddle, 1985
Hybrid tea • Moderate fragrance
Large plants • Large blooms

225

Scentimental
Carruth, 1996
Floribunda • Strong fragrance
Medium plants • Large blooms

Miss All-American Beauty
Meilland, 1965
Hybrid tea • Strong fragrance
Large plants • Very large blooms

Shadow Dancer
Moore, 1998
Climber • Slight fragrance
Large plants • Medium blooms

High Society
Zary, 2004
Climber • Moderate fragrance
Large plants • Large blooms

Miss Congeniality
Bédard, 2014
Grandiflora • Moderate fragrance
Medium plants • Medium blooms

Grande Dame
Carruth, 2010
Hybrid tea • Strong fragrance
Large plants • Large blooms

232

Fame!
Zary, 1998
Grandiflora • Slight fragrance
Medium plants • Large blooms

233

Benjamin Britten
Austin, 2002
Shrub • Moderate fragrance
Medium plants • Medium blooms

Perfume Delight
Swim/Weeks, 1973
Hybrid tea • Strong fragrance
Medium plants • Large blooms

Princess Alexandra of Kent
Austin, 2008
Shrub • Strong fragrance
Medium plants • Large blooms

Dee-Lish
Meilland, 2008
Hybrid tea • Strong fragrance
Large plants • Large blooms

Pretty Lady
Scrivens, 1996
Floribunda • Slight fragrance
Small plants • Large blooms

Parade Day
Bédard, 2017
Grandiflora • Strong fragrance
Medium plants • Large blooms

California Dreamin'
Meilland, 2009
Hybrid tea • Strong fragrance
Medium plants • Large blooms

Color Magic
Warriner, 1978
Hybrid tea • Moderate fragrance
Medium plants • Large blooms

The McCartney Rose
Meilland, 1991
Hybrid tea • Strong fragrance
Medium plants • Medium blooms

243

Jolie Veranda
Kordes, 2012
Floribunda • Slight fragrance
Small plants • Medium blooms

245

April in Paris
Zary, 2007
Hybrid tea • Strong fragrance
Medium plants • Large blooms

Julie Andrews
Delbard, 2020
Hybrid tea • Strong fragrance
Medium plants • Large blooms

Peter Mayle
Meilland, 2001
Hybrid tea • Strong fragrance
Medium plants • Large blooms

249

Social Climber
Jackson & Perkins, 2004
Climber • Moderate fragrance
Large plants • Large blooms

Tournament of Roses
Warriner, 1988
Grandiflora • Slight fragrance
Medium plants • Medium blooms

Tiffany
Lindquist, 1954
Hybrid tea • Strong fragrance
Medium plants • Large blooms

Memorial Day
Carruth, 2002
Hybrid tea • Strong fragrance
Medium plants • Large blooms

All Dressed Up
Bédard, 2018
Grandiflora • Slight fragrance
Large plants • Medium blooms

Marc Chagall
Delbard, 2015
Floribunda • Slight fragrance
Small plants • Medium blooms

259

Eden
Meilland, 1985
Climber • Slight fragrance
Large plants • Medium blooms

Bonica
Meilland, 1985
Shrub • Slight fragrance
Medium plants • Small blooms

263

Harlow Carr
Austin, 2005
Shrub • Strong fragrance
Medium plants • Large blooms

265

Jasmina
Kordes, 2006
Climber • Moderate fragrance
Large plants • Small blooms

Painted Porcelain
Bédard, 2020
Hybrid tea • Moderate fragrance
Medium plants • Small blooms

Passionate Kisses
Meilland, 1998
Floribunda • Slight fragrance
Medium plants • Medium blooms

270

Kathryn Morley
Austin, 1990
Shrub • Strong fragrance
Medium plants • Large blooms

Betty White
Meilland, 2002
Hybrid tea • Moderate fragrance
Medium plants • Large blooms

Scepter'd Isle
Austin, 1996
Shrub • Strong fragrance
Medium plants • Medium blooms

Queen of Sweden
Austin, 2005
Shrub • Moderate fragrance
Medium plants • Medium blooms

Wildeve
Austin, 2004
Shrub • Slight fragrance
Medium plants • Large blooms

Johann Strauss
Meilland, 1992
Floribunda • Moderate fragrance
Medium plants • Large blooms

Pink Enchantment
Kordes, 2009
Hybrid tea • Moderate fragrance
Medium plants • Medium blooms

Falling in Love
Carruth, 2006
Hybrid tea • Strong fragrance
Medium plants • Large blooms

283

Savannah
Kordes, 2014
Hybrid tea • Strong fragrance
Medium plants • Large blooms

Ballerina
Rearsby, 1997
Climber • Strong fragrance
Large plants • Small blooms

Candy Cane Cocktail
Meilland, 2016
Floribunda • Slight fragrance
Medium plants • Medium blooms

Perfume Breeze
Barni, 2007
Climber • Strong fragrance
Large plants • Small blooms

Mlle Cécile Brünner

Ducher, 1881
Old climber • Moderate fragrance
Large plants • Small blooms

Francis Meilland
Meilland, 2013
Hybrid tea • Strong fragrance
Large plants • Very large blooms

290

The Albrighton Rambler
Austin, 2014
Climber • Slight fragrance
Large plants • Small blooms

291

New Dawn
Dreer, 1930
Climber • Moderate fragrance
Large plants • Medium blooms

Stainless Steel
Carruth, 1991
Hybrid tea • Strong fragrance
Large plants • Large blooms

Florence Delattre
Guillot-Massad, 1997
Shrub • Strong fragrance
Medium plants • Medium blooms

Lavender Veranda
Kordes, 2014
Floribunda • Slight fragrance
Small plants • Small blooms

Arctic Blue
Bédard, 2018
Floribunda • Moderate fragrance
Medium plants • Large blooms

Love Song
Carruth, 2011
Floribunda • Slight fragrance
Medium plants • Medium blooms

298

299

Queen of Elegance
Bédard, 2019
Floribunda • Moderate fragrance
Medium plants • Large blooms

Paradise
Weeks, 1978
Hybrid tea • Strong fragrance
Medium plants • Large blooms

Neptune
Carruth, 2003
Hybrid tea • Moderate fragrance
Medium plants • Very large blooms

Easy to Please
Bédard, 2016
Floribunda • Moderate fragrance
Medium plants • Medium blooms

Royal Amethyst
DeVor, 1989
Hybrid tea • Moderate fragrance
Medium plants • Large blooms

Big Purple
Stephens, 1985
Hybrid tea • Strong fragrance
Medium plants • Large blooms

Heirloom
Warriner, 1972
Hybrid tea • Strong fragrance
Medium plants • Large blooms

Fragrant Plum
Christensen, 1990
Grandiflora • Strong fragrance
Medium plants • Large blooms

The Prince
Austin, 1993
Shrub • Strong fragrance
Small plants • Medium blooms

Young Lycidas
Austin, 2009
Shrub • Strong fragrance
Medium plants • Large blooms

Ebb Tide
Carruth, 2004
Floribunda • Strong fragrance
Medium plants • Large blooms

Heathcliff

Austin, 2013
Shrub • Strong fragrance
Medium plants • Large blooms

Intrigue
Warriner, 1982
Floribunda • Strong fragrance
Medium plants • Medium blooms

Celestial Night
Bédard, 2018
Floribunda • Slight fragrance
Medium plants • Medium blooms

William Shakespeare 2000
Austin, 2001
Shrub • Strong fragrance
Medium plants • Medium blooms

The Dark Lady
Austin, 1991
Shrub • Moderate fragrance
Medium plants • Medium blooms

Darcey Bussell
Austin, 2007
Shrub • Moderate fragrance
Medium plants • Medium blooms

Perfume Factory
Bédard, 2020
Hybrid tea • Strong fragrance
Medium plants • Medium blooms

Prospero
Austin, 1982
Shrub • Strong fragrance
Small plants • Medium blooms

Acknowledgments

There are so many people who have helped, supported, and guided my journey to Rose Story Farm and on to this book.

First and foremost, my husband, Bill: my partner in life and roses. We embarked on this journey together, learning and loving along the way. He is always positive, a glass-full kind of guy, encouraging, and extremely disciplined. He brings a more scientific and technical view to the table.

Patricia Dall'Armi, my mother. She instilled in me a love of roses, a respect for nature, and the knowledge that all things are possible, which I have passed on to my children. She lives with us on the farm now and is loved by all.

Nina Dall'Armi, my sister. She is invaluable in my life and career. Thank you for your 24/7 nonjudgmental support. I'm so lucky that she recently retired and is now working here on the farm full time.

A huge hug and thank-you to all my children for being a part of Rose Story Farm in different ways. You are my dearest loves.

A special thank-you goes to my youngest son, Geoffrey. He spent hours helping me with research, meticulous fact-checking, indexing, sorting, and imposing order where there was none.

Patti Keck, my business manager and so much more. Thank you for your constant voice of encouragement and sense of humor. She keeps the business moving forward. She has been pushing me to create this book since we began working together several years ago.

Victoria Pearson and I have worked together on rose projects for twenty-five years. The book is a dream come true for both of us. She is the only person who could have done this to my nitpicking standards. Every single photo shows the personality of the individual rose. Vicki is a tenacious perfectionist and above all a consummate professional. This book would not exist without her.

Aaron Pryor, Vicki's assistant was 100 percent invested in this book. He is calming, kind, and generous, and his creative input has been invaluable. Thank you for keeping us on track.

Otto & Sons nursery, run by the Klittich family, is *the* best rose nursery in the country. They grow out all of our new plants. Timmy Klittich led me on multiple early morning forays into their gardens and nursery, looking for rose blossoms to photograph. Andy Klittich was my sounding board for all things roses. Cindy Klittich was an invaluable second set of eyes on the photos. She knows her roses! And Scott Klittich tirelessly and generously shared everything he knows about roses, which is *a lot*. He is the ultimate rose guru. We have been swapping rose stories for the past twenty-five years.

My staff and friends at Rose Story Farm: Jorge Sanchez, Adriana Montelungo, Maria Mendoza, America Mejía, Jano and Tim Stack, and Bruce Blackwell keep our lives rosy, our fields alive with color, and always surround us with bouquets of the most beautiful colored blooms.

Claudio Cervantes and Rocelio Navarro are my go-to field workers on the farm. Their job was to find the perfect roses each morning to photograph. Their work was never easy but was always successful and done with grace and good humor.

Patricia Durham is a true friend and kept me from becoming too much of rose geek. She spent hours reading and rereading my book with the objective eyes of a layperson. Heather Dawn Miller's calm and steadfast confidence in me has been both invaluable and empowering.

Kim Curtis was my consultant on color and floral arranging and made sure all of my color choices were on point.

Leslie Stoker and Leslie Jonath, thank you for believing in me and bringing me this wonderful project.

Lisa Regul, thank you for having the vision for this book and making it a reality. Emma Campion worked tirelessly with me on the color sequencing in the book. I'm forever grateful for her patience and impeccable eye.

Amanda Poulsen Dix came late to the party but was invaluable to me. She was not only a pro at editing, but also contributed many inspirational ideas. She got the book on track, kept it there, and was a great addition to the team.

About the Contributors

Danielle Dall'Armi

Danielle Dall'Armi and Bill Hahn began Rose Story Farm in 1998 on their fifteen-acre farm in the Carpinteria Valley in Central California. Roses are not only their common passion but are the touchstone and foundation of their most enchanting and memorable experiences. The farm has more than 40,000 rose plants, cuttings from which supply the national floral trade and event design world. The farm also maintains a nursery with rose plants carefully curated for their garden clients. In addition, the farm offers a variety of seminars focused on garden design, rose cultivation, and flower arranging throughout the year.

Rose Story Farm and Danielle have been featured in *Wine Country Living*; *Santa Barbara Magazine*; *Sunset*; *Victoria* magazine; *O, The Oprah Magazine*; *Martha Stewart Living*; *Veranda*; the *Cottage Journal*; the *Wall Street Journal*; *Better Homes & Gardens*; *California Heartland*, a PBS special; NBC's *Today*; and Martha Stewart's online series *American Made*. Danielle has written and published articles in *American Rose*, the annual pub-

lication of the American Rose Society, on both flower arranging and garden design. Danielle is a frequent featured speaker at events that are focused on the beauty of the garden and the special role of roses in our daily lives.

Danielle's greatest honor was being selected as a "Great Rosarian of the World" in 2014. She joined an elite group of fifteen other recipients to receive this international award since its inception in 2001.

Victoria Pearson

A West Coast–based photographer, Victoria Pearson has worked in editorial, advertising, and commercial photography, shooting food, fashion, celebrities, gardens, travel destinations, still life, and interiors. Her work has appeared in many popular magazines, as well as advertising campaigns and cookbooks, including *Citrus: Sweet and Savory Sun Kissed Recipes* (Ten Speed Press). Victoria enjoys gardening and grows fruit trees, vegetables, herbs, and, of course, roses.

Index of Rose Names

Published in the United States by Ten Speed Press, an imprint of Random House,
a division of Penguin Random House LLC, New York.
TenSpeed.com
RandomHouseBooks.com

Ten Speed Press and the Ten Speed Press colophon are registered trademarks
of Penguin Random House LLC.

Typefaces: Fontsmith LTD's FS Kim and Swiss Typefaces' Euclid Circular B

Library of Congress Cataloging-in-Publication Data
Names: Dall'Armi Hahn, Danielle, 1953- author. | Pearson, Victoria, photographer.
Title: The color of roses : a curated spectrum of 300 blooms / Danielle Dall'Armi Hahn ;
    photographs by Victoria Pearson
Description: First edition. | Emeryville, California : Ten Speed Press,
    [2023] | Includes index.
Identifiers: LCCN 2022004651 (print) | LCCN 2022004652 (ebook) |
    ISBN 9781984861160 (hardcover) | ISBN 9781984861177 (ebook)
Subjects: LCSH: Rose gardens. | Roses. | Handbooks and manuals.
Classification: LCC SB411 .D25 2023 (print) | LCC SB411 (ebook) |
    DDC 635.9/33644—dc23/eng/20220218
LC record available at https://lccn.loc.gov/2022004651
LC ebook record available at https://lccn.loc.gov/2022004652

Hardcover ISBN: 978-1-9848-6116-0
eBook ISBN: 978-1-9848-6117-7

Printed in China

Editor: Lisa Regul | Production Editor: Joyce Wong
Cover design: Emma Campion | Lead designer: Nicole Sarry | Designer: Lisa Bieser
Art director: Emma Campion | Production designer: Mari Gill
Production and prepress color manager: Jane Chinn
Copyeditor: Andrea Chesman | Proofreader: Vicki Fisher
Marketer: Andrea Portanova

10 9 8 7 6 5 4 3 2 1

First Edition